The National Poetry Series was established in 1978 to ensure the publication of five collections of poetry annually through five participating publishers. The Series is funded annually by Amazon Literary Partnership, the Gettinger Family Foundation, Bruce Gibney, HarperCollins Publishers, Tabitha and Stephen King Foundation, Lannan Foundation, Newman's Own Foundation, Anna and Olafur Olafsson, Penguin Random House, the Poetry Foundation, Elise and Steven Trulaske, and the National Poetry Series Board of Directors.

2019 COMPETITION WINNERS

Little Big Bully
by Heid Erdrich of Minneapolis, MN
Chosen by Amy Gerstler for Penguin Books

Field Music
by Alexandria Hall of New York, NY
Chosen by Rosanna Warren for Ecco

Fractal Shores
by Diane Louie of Paris, France
Chosen by Sherod Santos for University of Georgia Press

Thrown in the Throat
by Benjamin Garcia of Auburn, NY
Chosen by Kazim Ali for Milkweed Editions

An Incomplete List of Names
by Michael Torres of Mankato, MN
Chosen by Raquel Salas Rivera for Beacon Press

THROWN IN
THE THROAT

BENJAMIN GARCIA

MILKWEED EDITIONS

Published 2020 by Milkweed Editions
Printed in Canada
Cover design by Mary Austin Speaker
Cover art by Benjamín García
20 21 22 23 24 5 4 3 2 1
First Edition

Milkweed Editions, an independent nonprofit publisher, gratefully acknowledges sustaining support from the Alan B. Slifka Foundation and its president, Riva Ariella Ritvo-Slifka; the Ballard Spahr Foundation; *Copper Nickel*; the McKnight Foundation; the National Endowment for the Arts; the National Poetry Series; the Target Foundation; and other generous contributions from foundations, corporations, and individuals. Also, this activity is made possible by the voters of Minnesota through a Minnesota State Arts Board Operating Support grant, thanks to a legislative appropriation from the arts and cultural heritage fund, and a grant from Wells Fargo. For a full listing of Milkweed Editions supporters, please visit milkweed.org.

Names: Garcia, Benjamin, 1987- author.
Title: Thrown in the throat : poems / Benjamin Garcia.
Description: First edition. | Minneapolis, Minnesota : Milkweed Editions, 2020. | Series: National poetry series | Summary: "Thrown in the Throat was selected for the 2019 National Poetry Series by Kazim Ali"-- Provided by publisher.
Identifiers: LCCN 2020017554 (print) | LCCN 2020017555 (ebook) | ISBN 9781571315212 (paperback ; acid-free paper) | ISBN 9781571319999 (ebook)
Subjects: LCGFT: Poetry.
Classification: LCC PS3607.A694 T48 2020 (print) | LCC PS3607.A694 (ebook) | DDC 811/.6--dc23
LC record available at https://lccn.loc.gov/2020017554
LC ebook record available at https://lccn.loc.gov/2020017555

Milkweed Editions is committed to ecological stewardship. We strive to align our book production practices with this principle, and to reduce the impact of our operations in the environment. We are a member of the Green Press Initiative, a nonprofit coalition of publishers, manufacturers, and authors working to protect the world's endangered forests and conserve natural resources. *Thrown in the Throat* was printed on acid-free 100% postconsumer-waste paper by Friesens.

CONTENTS

THROWN IN
THE THROAT

The Language in Question

The language in question is criminal // like a shark it ate a license plate // and it
ate the shark // well the fins it poached anyway // it gorges like a gorge // the river
flowing like a scarf some magician just keeps pulling // it ate away the deposits
of clay // like a sinkhole the language in question // ate a chateau and the family
inside // it pickpockets the stranger with gusto // it barters with bards // pays in
counterfeit // money is no object // the tongue desires // the language
acquires // the language in question likes conquest // moves west because it
hungers like locust // like the larvae of the caddis fly // this tongue makes a shell
of what it pilfered // it's the apex predator in the food pyramid // it ransacked the
pyramids // tours the spoils of theft to the country of origin // but only on
loan // a paper wasp that makes its home from what it chewed and spat back out of
your own // and it stings you if you get too close // too close // stung // I told you
the language in question is the S-shaped tongue of the anteater // the so-called
worm tongue // it warms itself at the fire it made from other people's
scrolls // codices // tomes // it entombs and embalms and lights bombs // the language
in question thinks it's Billy the Kid // the language in question is shooting up the
saloon // the language in question is shooting up meth // dope // coke // whatever's
on hand is the drug of choice // the language in question is corrupt // it's poison
and salve // savage and sage // it's honeysuckle and bitter oleander // only a lawyer
could make sense of it // and sell it to the highest bidder // like a snake that ate a
parrot whole // spits out the bright feathers // without a bird to hold them
together // that's what it's like when the accent doesn't even come close // the language
gets twisted // the tongue gets tired // I'd bet it's kinky and likes to be
tied // likes every bit of itself bit // this tongue bids adieu // holed in the
mouth // ah-dee-ose // ah-mee-goes

Warrior Song

after Robert Pinsky

When our mothers had no water for themselves
we drank. When we had no bed we mapped a plot
in the dirt. We had to lie in the dirt of your country.

When we had no money we worked.
When we had no license we walked.
When we had no strength our mind kept walking.

When we had no passport our blood
was our passport. When there was no train
we hauled the weight of our own body.

When we had no companion we remembered
God is our companion. When we had no
direction our family was our compass.

When we had no faith luck
was our faith. When we have finished
death will be our luck.

Undocumented is our status, resistance
is our cause. Because we cannot sleep
we dream with open eyes.

Averting the Gaze

mom didn't know I was gay
because she chose not to see
like the maidens of Pompeii
that were instead two boys
we'd now call gay we found
in a last embrace his head
on his chest we might change
our minds about who can hug
who and girls might be boys
people don't stop being people
like the iis at the end of Pompeii
all on their own tongues do things
without us when we aren't looking
the least of which is holding hands

On the Slight Cruelty of Mothers

Just look at these hands, holding my small palms in hers. *They have never had to work a day in their life!* She spit into one, shut the other over, rubbed them together, and with her hands on my wrists made me comb my hair in place. *You want to be a handsome boy.*

//

I brought her a pink rose, but in one pull she stripped off all the petals and made me hold out my hands, palm-side down. I thought she might strike them. Instead, she licked one petal after another, placing them on my fingernails. *I could do this all day when I was a girl.*

//

And when I watered her roses, she snuck up behind me, slipped a stem between her middle and ring finger, like a wineglass, stroking with her thumb the near-open bud: *wouldn't you like to have a dress as wonderful as a rose petal? Well, not you,* digging her thumbnail into the flesh. *But that would be something.*

Eye of the Hurricane

Garcia is my common name, but you can call me by my suborder:
　　Vermilingua, because my tongue worms into pockets. *¿Quieres*
　　　　ver mi lengua? If you want to keep America America, better bolt it
　　　　　　down or lock it. *Ahí vamos.*

An anteater isn't afraid of a cage, won't hesitate to smite, transforms
　　its tropical depression to a migration
　　　　of wrath, machetes down its own path, though it contains
　　　　　　in its craw, a rainbow—un arco iris.

If you choose, you can crawl away from this, if
　　you brunt the gridlock and contraflow
　　　　on I-45 North, along the evacuation route.
　　　　　　There is an out

though disaster is never complete. Without you,
　　the domestic animal left inside
　　　　the house might still survive.
　　　　　　Though you are embarrassed by something

smaller than a crushed ant, the shit stains of cockroaches,
　　pocking the spine of your English
　　　　texts, the edges of your spiral notebooks.
　　　　　　A tongue isn't worth very much,

but there is enough for everyone. Remember: there is no cage;
　　you cannot leave; the joke: *why do Mexicans wear pointy boots?*
　　　　To get the roaches in the corners.
　　　　　　We all had German,

American, whatever kind of cockroach
        shitting on our books, in our alarm clocks telling us to go the fuck
             to school, where with difficulty,
                        I learned in drills

to kneel in single file along hard and polished halls
        where the floor confronts the wall, then cover my ears
             as the storm roared above. My class was promised
                    a piece of hard candy

to complete this analogy: tire : hubcap :: hurricane : _____. *You*
        keep those grades up, one day you're going to make so much money.
             So why do Mexicans wear pointy boots? I didn't
                    delouse my tongue, because even then,

I knew. Nothing comes quickly but disaster. I would have to make myself
        fat on what others might be made sick by. *But where is your family*
        really from? What's your native tongue?
                I ate it—

Ode to the Corpse Flower

In the language of flowers // I am the one who says // fuck you
I won't be anyone's nosegay // this Mary is her own // talking bouquet

never let a man speak for you or call you // what he wants // I learned that
the hard way // amorphophallus titanum // it sure sounds pretty in a dead tongue

except it's Latin for big ugly dick // I mean I am // but what an asshole scientist
I prefer to think of myself // & this may sound vain // as a goddess

cadaver dressed in drag // my stage name // Versace Medusa
part Lilith part calla lily // keep your heteronormative birds & bees // give me

the necrophiliacs // the freaks the meat-eating // beetle & flesh fly
there I go again allies // getting all hot & bothered // being vulgar

vulgar meaning common // as when something is below you // like a girl
forbidden to say fuck // it makes a woman sound so common // oh come on

that's all you expect from a flower // to be likeable // but to keep it raw & 100
is to be abhorred // fine but even the haters will pay // to hold their nose

at a halftime show // they'll claim they are beyond Beyoncé // sick of Selena
yet they can't look away from the Live Cam // no one wants to miss // the showgirl

as she breaks through the cake // unhooks her lingerie // La Virgen de Guadalupe
with a twist of Santa Muerte // what in the hell is she wearing // glad you ask

death is the new Christian Dior // the latest Chanel is corpse smell // I am the week-old
ham hock whore of horticulture // I bring the hothouse haute couture // & I always come

in last place // dressed to the nines I get what I want // which is to be The Tenth Muse
Sor Juana Inés de la Cruz // little Evita de Buenos Aires // screwing & screwing over

los descamisados on my Rainbow Tour // fuck Whitman fuck Pound // give me Emily D
speaking of which have I ever told you daddy // only sun gods get me hard // you want it

I got it // let me show you how a chola really leans // mother nature may wear floral
but I ain't your mama // I thirst like Betty Boop at peak coquette // Marilyn Monroe

blowing in an air vent // say Malinche say Truvadawhore // give me more
I thrive in shade // my throat is my throne so // queen me bitch

The Language in Question

He has a mouth on him. Yes, bitch.
But allow me this amendment:
I've had several mouths on me,
sometimes simultaneously, but let's
not go there now. Suffice it to say
God gave me two ears & one mouth
for reasons I've been unconvinced by.
Goddamn, my mouth has many uses:
eat, sing, bite, kiss, but most of all
insinuate. Have you ever been sucked
by the cups of an octopus's underside?
It's a daily special I highly recommend
to the critics who might say some words
don't belong in poems. Just because
you won't twirl the legs of a live octopus
due to texture or fear of asphyxiation
doesn't mean it won't taste good. Taste
is what the octopus does on its way down
with its tentacles. The language in question
is like that. It's a squishy, worm-like squirm,
can contort and go down the wrong pipe.
If some words don't belong in poems, then
I say some people can go fuck themselves.
Just kidding, I don't really say that because
they might actually enjoy it, if they could only
let themselves relax. Here's a word I never
thought I'd have occasion to use in a poem:
poppers. One whiff and even a no-vice novice
could let the sphincter open just long enough
for this octopus to pass: uvula violet vulva.

Heroin with an E

for Marlene Garcia

//

you might do well // to learn the other uses
of an opium poppy // pick one and flip it
upside down // it's a doll in a bright red dress
but where is her head // where is her head
strip the flower // petals bunched together
like a clump of hair // oxygen rich scrunchie
on a sideways ponytail // pin the flower head
to your blouse // now it's a homecoming mum
that night // you didn't come home to mom
didn't want to become a mom // so you pressed
the poppy between your thighs // a cup of seeds
something called a diaphragm // you liked it so
you did it again // no one told you how good
it could feel // stay away just don't do it say no
you took another hit // because goddamn all of it
plucked & plucked he loved you & loved you // not
flower head tossed in the toilet // a blood clot
with an ovum caught inside it // because fuck him

//

is that unpleasant to your palate // then pick another
poppy by the stem // and take a light to it on either end
it bleeds a white ash // your mother in the kitchen
waiting & waiting measuring her life // in cigarettes
and coffee spoons she burns // the slender neck of a poppy
it's the incense smoking in the hallway // praying
the myrrh might pry you from // whatever traphouse
you're calling home tonight // dull halo of dust
where the kitchen TV was // where you were once
entranced by the Technicolor // Emerald City Oz
you were just a girl and couldn't help but fall // asleep
before Dorothy even reached // the nodding flowers
dusk fielding the sepia window // where *are* you
I never worry about your brothers // married and working
and working and why aren't you // calling home tonight
she watches the window like a TV channel // bad connection
turn the dial jiggle the wire // snow still cuts the picture
why aren't you aren't you calling home // home tonight

//

when all of what had to have happened // happened
when I slept on the floor of a street // mother called
rock bottom // when I thought I couldn't fall deeper
I rolled into the gutter // I fell and fell into the sewer
I swam against the slurry // it felt like I would kick & kick
and it's like I wasn't moving // in a tango called the 12 step
God was my partner and he wouldn't lead // had two left feet
I'm going to drown down here is that what you want // no
I still have two feet left I said // God said you got this girl
that's when I stopped fighting // it's called accepting
what we cannot change // I rode the current to the end
of a sewage treatment plant // I was treated and cycled

through vats of waste // pushed through grates my hair
caught in the spinning filters // chemical and electrolysis
processed // any minute in jail is another minute alive
my mother said this and it must be // the most generous
use of that term mother // the voice of God was obnoxious
he said Marlene bitch you got this // why me why me Lord
even light can be a kind of pollution even sound // sulfur
makes the eternal waters of some lakes // clear as death
and still life breeds there // if you dare to call that living
methadone suboxone maintenance // so what if you need this
the difference between drug and medicine // is why you take it
take it every day every day // you think your life is worthless
remember that // sometimes even a diamond was once alive

Le daría mis pulmones

Toward the end, she could only
lift a cup of coffee. Closer still,
even that became too much for her,
my mother. A sponge, then,
I'd dip in coffee, or pan dulce,
and put that to her lips to suck. That
was all the cancer let her manage.

The IV was her sugar water, and she
the hummingbirds she loved to watch,
busy at the red and yellow feeder.
Those plastic flowers welded on
were poor excuses, but they worked. Whatever

worked, I guess, my mother thought,
lived. On the bed in the living room,
her body of sleeping birds, her dream
of a thousand green wings shimmering like
shreds of aluminum, that could, at any moment,
unloose on the wind. Toward

the end, the sponge and the coffee, the cancer.
She couldn't smoke anymore either, of course,
because even drawing her own drag: impossible.
So she had me smoke for her—nine years old—
I was her lungs. I blew the smoke right in her face, right
in her face. Just like that, over and over:

To the Unborn Sibling

Small and angry towns pock this section of HWY 287 that skewers clear across the fat gut of Texas, and our father won't stop for anything but gas. No armadillo is safe. The one time we did stop for food, the owner refused, even though us kids could translate the orders. So if you don't want to piss in a can or you lack that equipment or you think the metal mouth of the can will bite, hold it until we stop for gas. Because our oldest brother, caught off guard by a bump in the road, perhaps a pothole or unlucky creature, cut himself you-know-where. That's why we call him the Castrato. And boy, do nicknames stick. Our other brother: Wetpants. Take it from me, no matter how many changes of clothes, he will never dry. And as for me, I have been left behind before, and that's all it takes to know what those little Texas flags mean, that white star like cotton breaking the pod, the open throat of a cottonmouth.

Reasons for Abolishing Ice '

with a first line by Bei Dao

because the ice age is over now   ice
because this isn't our first winter   ice
because the polar caps are melting   ice
because hands up if they say freeze   ice
because it's getting hard to breathe   ice
because it feels like walking on glass   ice
because crops are rotting in the field   ice
because it's clear it won't last forever   ice
because it looks like a diamond but isn't   ice
because you are here to take our people   ice
because I think we know enough of hate   ice
because we're gathering around the fire   ice
because snowflakes also cause whiteouts   ice
because you took the people out of police   ice
because I see you——I see you——I see you   ice
because black is considered more dangerous   ice
because they say the polar caps aren't melting   ice
because a person could slip through at any moment   ice
because you say we can't use our voice to launch an avalanche ice
because if you want papers then we'll crush you like booklice thumbed into paper

Mourning Dove

One shot through the neck was all it took for the dove to go down flat. No flit, not even the tinge of a note. A clean kill, a real beauty. The bird filled my two palms up whole with its body. At the end of my fingers, the neck dipped back, eyes semi-open. And blood dribbled out in rubies.

This close, her eyelids looked larger than I would have imagined. My mother's eyes were like that the last time I saw her—someone had powdered gunpowder blue eye shadow to shadow the bruising. She never wore makeup, and now she would never wake up to take it off. A stray bullet sounds as harmless as a stray dog until that dog has you in its jaws.

Ten years old, I took it to my father who worked on the front porch stripping electrical cord from the plastic case, revealing a copper redder than any new minted penny. He would noose one end to the post and scrape as he walked along the yards of wire with his old skinning knife.

Dad looked at the creature in my hands. Then he studied my hands, tracing with his eyes along my arms/chest/neck/face. He asked why I killed such a beautiful thing. I kept silent. He put down his knife and walked to the trash. *Come here and I'll teach you what my daddy taught me.*

He snatched patches of feathers by pinching his fingers and pulling hard. *Hold the bird using only your left hand. Pin the head down good with your thumb. Grab a few feathers with your free hand, then pull up and away from your body—like you're lighting a match. Got that?*

I nodded.

Do it 'til the bird is clean, weighing it lightly in one hand as if on a scale. *This won't be enough. Keep shooting or she will have died for nothing,* as he handed me the body.

A Father's Portrait in Styrofoam

Spun of almost nothing
and yet we don't know,
actually, if it will return,
like a father gone for milk,
to the nothing it still is.
That cliché won't decay
or ripen. It makes a nice life
jacket, I'll say that much.
Yeah, he made a nice life
out west, in Vegas, I've heard. If
Hidalgo means the son of something,
then I am the son of almost
nothing—Styrofoam.
That which gets gotten rid of
without going away.
In that respect, my father
is also like a cockroach.
If the desert can't nuke him,
nothing will. He's insular,
disposable; he's a man's
man, in fact, he's a manufactured
tumbleweed. He's resistant
to rot, he's stubborn, he's
soft—he's so soft my child's hand
could crush his skull like a tulip.
But be careful, with that one, son,
I sense there's a scorpion
trapped beneath a Dixie cup.

Conversations with My Father // A Poem in Closet Verse

When was the last time
you took a girl to the movies?

                                    //

                        It's been a long time
                        since I've seen a movie.

You should marry
a pretty girl in Albuquerque.

                                    //

                        I don't think I'm ever
                        moving back to Albuquerque.

God wants us to the know the joy
of being a father.

                                    //

                        Maybe God doesn't want me
                        to be a father.

When will you be a father,
like me?

                                    //

                        Having children doesn't make a father,
                        at least not to me.

I mean, I would like it if you made me
a grandfather again.

                                    //

                        You either are or you aren't.
                        There is no again.

Ode to the Peacock

In the language of handkerchiefs // there's really nothing // I don't want
I'm glad to be paid in gold // when the devil beats his // you know what

if you think it's indecent // for a body to fan open iridescent // gird your gaze
because honey I'm throwing up // my kerchief like a flare gun shot // watch me

unskirt a frosted muffin // top me with sprinkles // I'm flashing red-yellow-green-go
you're the stallion and I'm the mare // smear my queer into the mirror // now you

are the mare and I am // the stale smell in the restroom stall // and you're an all-
you-can-eat buffet // let me say your eyes are the most beautiful // urinal cake blue

blew as in the past tense of blow // blow as in coke even though you // suck it up
buttercup and butterscotch // a man named Scott wants his scotch // filthy gorgeous

or maybe that's a martini // a man named Martin a man named // who knows what
who knows what it means to pluck roses // from my chest // using just his teeth

and sometimes yes blood // which is thicker than water // I know something thicker
it's called incest // when a nephew makes his uncle say uncle // say pee say cock

Katy Perry sings the song // let me see your peacock-cock // behold my royal flesh
stamped with eyes // don't tiptoe in your slippers // stomp on eggs shells balloons

lick my boots until I see myself // being spit on like // you're squelching the inferno
sometimes fire sometimes feathers // elect a whip or bind me // blind in leather

pink polka dot and seafoam green // if you don't already know // let me show you what it means for a boy to be // a boy-to-be // when hard in my harness you'd best

call me daddy // but don't call any of this dirty // not unless the person doing it wants it then it's smut // wipe the rosary from my brow // use the fabric pouring from your lips

This Way to the Egress

"At one point, Barnum noticed that people were lingering too
long at his exhibits. He posted signs indicating 'This Way to the
Egress'. Not knowing that 'Egress' was another word for 'Exit',
people followed the signs to what they assumed was a fascinating
exhibit—and ended up outside."
—WIKIPEDIA

With a name like that, it could be a bald baby
female eagle, an eaglet, but "this way to the egress"
is another way of getting told *get out* without
being crass. Fancy it a word trick, now use it
in a sentence: "Because of past factory fires,
every room by code should have one door
and a second means of egress." Like this,
my patriotic ignorance of history is an eaglet
of regret, fed on the dead fish the mother stole
from other birds, in a behavior known to us
as parasitism. Though it sounds like parrotivism,
or what a parrot does when it copies us. But a bird
can't understand language in the fullest sense,
only in a full-ish sense. Let me repeat here
what I was told as a child: Benjamin Franklin
despised the eagle as a national symbol.
He favored the turkey, for its self-reliance.
I don't know if this is true, but in that America,
no bill would pass if it meant trickery, to take
from another. But I digress, this way to the…

The Darkest Lashes

A wrought iron fence in her
             gaze. She jumps it to save
                          ten minutes walking home

after work. I slip through the bars.
             If you think she is a doe, don't
                          mistake her for a doe. Don't

forget, that is the summer
             she would teach you to be the mother
                          of the baby chicks whose mother

we ate—grinding hard, raw rice
             with our teeth, letting the young peck
                          from the tips of our own tongues.

She is tired from sacking potatoes.
             School is out, I couldn't be more
                          than six years old, tired of walking.

Carry me, I say. Her arm belts my waist,
             pressed against her, stomach to stomach. She says,
                          Así, como un costal de papas.

The train yard's fence shrinks behind us
             to the size of a man's comb. I am ashamed
                          of eating potatoes and my mother,

an ordinary laborer. I didn't know
             what hunger was then. Memory is quick to
                          whip me for what I did and didn't do.

The Memory Jar

Sister, you will ask yourself, twelve years from now, the rest
of your life, why, as you slept, your little brother poured
a whole jar of June beetles into the tangled nest of your hair.

Remember the time you sat me pantless on an anthill or
when you locked me overnight in the chicken coop.
How you tricked me into picking prickly pear
barehanded.

Remember it, remember.

The more you pull, the tighter the grip.
Each beetle cleaving six fishhook legs.
Each blessed, shit-eating scarab
hissing and spitting at you like the harlot
you are in a book I've not yet read but will.

It won't be for three days
the last bug leg falls out.
I have ruined your birthday forever.

And still you are ungrateful. You can't be bothered
to think of what your brother went through for you.
Dark hours in the yard the night before, waiting
by the one porch light, offering my body freely
to the mosquitoes as I hand-selected the choice beetles—
only those whole and larger than a quarter. I treated

each and every scarab with utmost care,
and just before I would place them in the jar,
brought each hissing bug an inch from my lips
and whispered:

    she hates you, she hates you.

Queso de patas

güera they called my mother,
        whitest of seven siblings,
                though she was never white as snow

or milk—her skin tinged amber
        like the Mexican cheese that smelled of feet
                that I refused to eat as a child, convinced

the cheese was mixed
        by rancher's bare toes, like grapes
                mashed to make some tawny wine

and from brown and cracked soles
        acquired its yellow color, inherited
                the yellow skin, odorous hard wheel

that did not melt, only crumbled when fresh
        or aged would shred upon metallic scales
                to sawdust or confetti strands that,

when sprinkled, exhaled a pungent breath
        of naked feet that have kissed the earth,
                stroked bare cement floors, caressed the skin

of other feet, and from contact grown callused
        but beautiful, that if covered must breathe
                through open-toed shoes—huaraches, *that*

was my mother, the güera needing air
    and when her flesh was tossed into the melting
        pot, she resisted, the strength of callused soles,

hard, ungrated as she tread upon this foreign soil
    barefoot an acquired taste that if you smelled
        and did not eat, you could not understand

The Language in Question

When I called you a beluga whale, I meant it
as a compliment. *What a noble beast.* You said this to me,
meaning me. Maybe I'm wrong, but I'm starting to think
that this comparison is not without its faults. I was wrong
in bed when I grabbed your belly fat, and I said it wasn't fat
but my hand adrift in sensory deprivation. Total a-hole move,
but it did remind me of my own body's buoyancy. As a boy,
I grew up near the sea, and my mother would say
una mujer le da sal a su hombre, you just remember that
not knowing if she meant that salt can halt earth's growth
or tongue man's junk to pearl. When my mother left,
my father ate a box of Morton salt hoping he would die.
He didn't die and I called you a beluga whale and I'm sorry
you're salty because you think belugas are dopey dolphins—
but did you know they train their masters and not vice versa?
Belugas blow hoops of bubbles like smoke rings off a cigar
right into the trainer's face, and the sub smiles at his dom,
won like a cheap prize at the ring toss. Oh! And scientists
actually recorded them mimicking human speech! Ask them
how they know it wasn't just clicks or squeals or noise,
they'll say: because it fell within *our own* acoustical spectrum.
One beluga was singing, another appeared to be yelling
out, out, out! Mimicking human speech, like humans at the zoo
telling the chimp *stop, stop, stop* while it hurls fistfuls of poop.
This all started when you asked me: *what is my animal spirit?!*
Don't forget. It doesn't work like that. You don't get to choose
who you fall in love with. But I am trying to be a noble beast.
I have been practicing white people speech for years and years.
Forgive me. I was always about to understand you.

The Great Glass Closet

This is not a metaphor: when I say that I lived in the closet, it's because I lived in the closet.

You might, too, if you shared a one-bedroom apartment with eleven other people and a pet: mother, stepfather, brother, brother, brother, uncle, aunt, cousin, cousin, cousin, cousin, dog. Then there's me, the surplus.

You could have called our closet a walk-in closet in the sense that a child's body could walk in. Mine did, and I called it home. It was comfortable enough, if you were willing to lie. I was.

//

I lived in a confession booth, listening to my own secrets, making my own sentences.

Confession: my uncle was different in a way you could see.
          I was different in a way you could see

only if you were looking.
    If you were looking, I could see.

What I mean is that my uncle walked on crutches, so he couldn't cross the border by foot. He climbed into the trunk of a car, which is a kind of closet.

I was like my uncle, and I was not like my uncle. He walked on crutches and I didn't.

Confession: during prayers, I don't close my eyes. Nobody knows this except the other people who don't close their eyes.

//

A life in the closet is a life that's closed, so I opened what I could—books. I was Harry Potter, The Boy Who Lived, reading about The Boy Who Lived.

I had no owl, no hat, no wand. I couldn't cast a spell, and I couldn't spell. But I could see the *low* in *owl*, I could pull the *hat* out of *that*, and in the word *wand* find another hidden *and*.

Reading X-Men, I wanted to be Storm so that I could end the famine in my family's village, looking like a badass bitch/queen/goddess doing it. I knew this was impossible because I wasn't claustrophobic enough. I could never be Storm.

I survived too many storms behind a closet door. And I could never change my name to Storm, which at its core contains an *or*. As in, either/or. As in, Ororo Monroe—Storm's birth name.

You must choose:
  pink or blue, boy or girl, left or right, right or wrong, truth or lie, truth or dare.

Truth: even writing this I thought that feminine shared an *a* with famine—*femanine*. Dare: hunger for errors, find another place to stick a *man* inside.

Reading, I learned the difference between *cloth* and *clothe*. Also the difference between *close* meaning *to shut*, and *close*, meaning *almost there*.

//

Sometimes there's no difference between the past and present, as in: *to read* and *to have read*.

Sometimes there's no difference between the past and present except for the surroundings. You can call this context or you can call this what it is—privilege. Not living in the closet is what people like me did on TV.

But I wasn't like the people on TV, so I lived in the closet.

//

In *Fun Home,* when Alison and her father see a woman wearing men's clothes and sporting a man's haircut, she says:

"Like a traveler from a foreign country who runs into someone from home—someone they've never spoken to, but know by sight—I recognized her with a surge of joy."

"Dad recognized her, too."

Spoiler alert: Alison and her father were both in the closet, but they were not in the closet together.

//

My room was a closet for my family's clothes, my clothes were a closet for my skin, my skin is a closet for my skeleton. It won't always be.

It won't always be this way,
                    but that's not the same as "it gets better."

Better requires context:

                    a shell could be a spent bullet or the home of a mollusk.

In order to breathe, you have to add the little snail of an *e* to the end of the word *breath*.

Breathe. Is it not amazing that we are still alive?

//

It's nothing amazing, but in the closet is where I first read *The Voyages of Doctor Doolittle*. Marooned on Spider Monkey Island, the only way Tommy can go home is to climb inside the pink shell of the Great Glass Sea Snail.

I lived in the closet—all wall, no window. So that if I turned out the light, it made no difference if I shut my eyes. That's how dark it got.

I used to pretend I was Tommy inside the enormous shell—all window, no wall. But what was there to see at the bottom of the sea? Nothing except rare animals that learned, under great pressure, to make light from nothing but the nothing that they are.

It was cold down there. And lonely. My breath would fog the shell until I wiped it clear.

But I climbed in when the Great Glass Sea Snail bowed its great neck to me and let me enter, hoping I had enough air, heading straight for whatever waited on the next shore,

      like any immigrant would.

A Toast to the Destruction of Sodom and Gomorrah

The waitress tending our party of three dips her tanned
torso over the table as she grabs the menus from us men. Well,

> men minus one, since it appears that I'm the only guy
> not looking. Not looking at women anyway. The gold

crucifix on her necklace rubs against my brother's straw
as she withdraws and Jesus ascends again to the heaven

> of her breasts. The Motorboat is what I order, described
> as something between a porter and a stout—now that's

my kind of cross. My father says there's no such thing as sin
that's large and sin that's small. Drinking too much, he says,

> is the sin, not the drinking, as he peers through our waitress'
> gingham crop top. There's no such thing as small or large

sizes here, the waitress says, man-size is large, girl is small.
Do you really want to order the girl-size? Fine, I want the girl-

> size. My brother laughs and my father looks away. It's stupid,
> my brother says. But are you really telling me her body

did nothing for you? My father looks at me like God
looking for the smallest redemption in Gomorrah, looking

> for any reason in Sodom not to raze it. There is no reason
> for how things are sometimes—better to accept. My father

didn't raise me to be a girly man, a fact that might bother him,
except for the other fact: he didn't raise me. It bothers him.

        Some people are beyond saving. Me, I tell my brother, as I look
      over his shoulder at the bearded roughneck going gaga

for our waitress as he sips from his bottle, there is nothing
straight about me, except maybe my hair, and even that

        has gotten kinky with age. I drink beer because I'm thirsty
      eating salted pretzels. I don't have a prayer when I say amen.

Ode to the Pitcher Plant

In the Victorian language of fans // como se dice // come hither
I am the three-headed // head giver // Heather Heather and Heather

be my Veronica Sawyer // but you'll have to dye // your virgin hair
let me make you over // a quien le importa if they say // she's a man-

eater // they're not wrong about the latter // I expect a booty call later
from my whereforeartthou Romeo // come use my trellis as a ladder // I am

pansexual // with omnivore vigor make you breakfast // the morning after
see me wavering // waving my spade impatiently // for any lad or lass

to come shake that ass // booty-bump-a-bump // let me whet your appetite
with my siren waters // seamen // which is what a man's come is called

I want a man // that comes when called // I want to have a better name
for when women climax // meanwhile my secret is vaginal // secretions

gender fluids and fluid genders // see how come can mean // collapse
of distance between objects // to the point of overlap // until two are one

as is the case with come // love // in Spanish those four letters mean come eat
they fold into each other // like a hand fan // *come* you're almost skin and bones

and meat and legs and wings and // carapace // cara mia come at your own pace
but come // down my throat follow your gut to my gut // come Narcissus come

to your sissy prissy boipussy pitcher // I'll be your catcher too // the game is lost
my fans are in the stands // doing the wave they're cheering you on // come on

roll your love into a ball // if we had but world enough and time // I would woo you
to kingdom come // but life's a stuff will not endure // so gift me your endurance

damelo duro papi // forgo coquetry's etiquette // I've got your ticket down here
where bodies float // transverse the manhole cover // draw the curtain and do

mind the man behind // I'm flashing my fan as hard as I can // ready for my close up
I am the Victor with a capital V // thank you for your participation here's // a trophy

Mutual Monogamy

The key term is *mutual*, which implies a reciprocal relationship, the way 6 is to 9. Although mutually monogamous usually means missionary, as in, a tuxedoed Mr. launching the arrow of his [r] between her [M] and [s.] after a long run of near misses. Mutually monogamous = only us, 1+1, it's considered a closed system—no one can get in or out. And when no one can get in or out we call that a jail cell. It's true, this method can prevent disease because you can't give each other something you don't have. But a relationship is like trying to put two halves of an orange back together: you have to keep holding them there or else they fall apart. Mutually monogamous insists a couple can't be split in two for the same reason you can't cut a hole in half. Because there's no such thing as half a hole. A hole can only be made deeper, like a well, or filled in, like a grave. Because you can't give each other something you don't have, sometimes people step outside of their relationships. It's a terrible thing to plunge in a well or be buried alive. On the other hand, having sex with other people is like passing love notes between bodies. That's how HIV slides a letter opener into the slit of a white envelope or syphilis screws its way subsurface. In jail, one of the few pleasures is writing and receiving letters. You can choose to be mutually monogamous or not (that's on you), but *shhh*, keep it to yourself whatever you do.

Nonmonogamy

What's in a name I can't say, but—and this is just a guess—even if a rose did smell as sweet by any other, I'm willing to bet a shitballsnotflower would garner fewer gardens. There is something like a word inside a word in names. Take for example the word *know*. To know someone is another way to say you fucked. You can deny it, n—o sits in the middle and who knows what k and w are doing. Jiggle a letter here, and slide a letter there, and get rid of what is silent. You get the word own. And to be thoroughly fucked is to get owned. Meanings under meanings are called subtext, and words under words are called lies. I might sleep with twelve-hundred men, but who could know me more than you?

Bliss Point or What Can Best Be Achieved by Cheese

A.k.a.
　　　　the other gold.
　　　　　　Now that's the stuff,
　　　　　　　　shredded or melted
　　　　　　　　　　or powdered
　　　　　　　　　　　　or canned.
　　　　　　　　　　　　　　Behold
　　　　　　　　the pinnacle of man
　　　　　in a Cheeto puff!
Now that's the stuff
　　　　　you've been primed for:
　　　　　　　　fatty & salty & crunchy
　　　and poof—gone. There's the proof.
Though your grandmother
　　　　　never even had one. You can't
　　　　　have just one. You
　　　　　　　inhale them puff—
　　　　　　　　　　　　after puff—
　　　　　　　　　　after puff—
　　　　　You're a chain smoker. Tongue
　　　coated & coaxed
but not saturated or satiated.
　　　　It's like pure flavor,
　　　　　　but sadder. Each pink ping
　　　　　　　in your pinball-mouth
　　　　　　　　　　expertly played
　　　　　by the makers who have studied you,
　　　　the human animal, and culled
　　from the rind
your Eve in the shape
　　　　of a cheese curl.

Girl,
come curl in the dim light of the TV.
Veg out on the verge of no urge
of anything.
Long ago we beached ourselves,
climbed up the trees then
down the trees,
knuckled across the dirt
& grasses & thorns & Berber carpet.
Now is the age of sitting,
so sit.
And I must say,
crouched on the couch like that,
you resemble no animal.
Smug in your Snuggie and snug
in your sloth, you look
nothing like a sloth.
And you are not an anteater,
an anteater eats ants
without fear
of diabetes. Though breathing,
one could say, resembles a chronic disease.
What's real
cheese and what is cheese product?
It's difficult to say
but being alive today
is real-
real-
really
like a book you can't put down, a stone
that plummets from a great height. Life's
a "page-turner" alright.
But don't worry

if you miss the finale
        of your favorite show, you can
                catch it on queue. Make room
for me and I'll binge on this,
                    the final season with you.

Anti-Ode to the Man-of-War

In the language of hormones // I want to say // I'm sorry
that you don't know // the gulf between the words // venom

and poison // between // the father the son & the holy
crap I just got stung // let me explain myself // enzymes

are my hello // goodbye // I've been told I have a terminal case
of resting bitch face // the facts // there is a difference between

venom & poison // it's all about who // is doing what to whom
bite me // and it's called a poison // venom when I bite back

this is what wars have been // fought over // in the holy name of
whose key is unlocking // whose keyhole // another way to think

of them is venoms // are the tops // they're active and push in
while poisons are the bottoms // the tubers the roots // the locks

of hemlock-haired // fuck boys // the cads & the rent-to-owns
you know how I know // you're a poison // it's cause you're lazy

daisy & docile // I lift my sail a while // and why not be
the Portuguese // armored warship // that's my namesake

I am small & still // I contain multitudes // I wonder if Whitman
might have meant // dudes he knew // husked & hulled & filled

his debonair // crowned with windswept hair so // devil-may-care
unlikely though it may seem // I'm not the jealous // kind of fish

even if I may not be // kind to you // pain's the only way I know
flesh from friend // you know a relationship is extra // toxic when

one dolt is left stunned // defenselessly doting // no thanks I am
like the Iberian newt // that would rather push his ribs // through

his own skin // to deliver the venom than // let a man touch me
that's really fucked // but I don't know any other joke // except

how does one hug // a box jellyfish // the punchline is you don't
I bet you didn't // think this was love // poetry when it started

it isn't // except I don't know any other way // to love or to be
loved but for this // I want to be done with you & you // with me

do what the men of war do // to the ripped torso // of the surfer
I won't let you suffer // alone & not for long // I want to do

with you what I've been told // human urine // does to the fists
of pink hydrangeas // in the spring // before the blue blooming

Birds of Illegal Trade

To be a traitor is to trade—
      Take, for example, the blue macaw

of my childhood, traded
      for two rocks of crack

and a dime of blow. My block raided
      each week by waves of drive-bys,

waves of cops, while I sprayed Raid
      on roaches, white powder on fire

ant mounds, bedbugs, though nothing aided.
      Into Houston's Fifth Ward

the hyacinth macaw was added,
      intensely blue as is allowed

only to Crips and royalty. I felt like a traitor
      just to behold it, tied to the T

of a laundry post, misty canopy traded
      for a man's pit-stained shirts strung

on a line. My brothers and I would have raided
      the house if we could, taught the bird

more than cuss words. The owner stated,
      my pit bull's gonna eat your face

if I catch you here again. The bird ate it,
  the medley of banana and guava

from our own front yard. The image hasn't faded:
  a royal blue macaw—lazuli, cobalt,

sapphire, none of these would I have traded
  for the view through my chain-link fence,

clutching the rusted wire diamonds—added
  to my mind like a cigarette goes through

a T-shirt, like the sun, visible though bated,
  reaches the forest floor. Siren lights

whirled their blue as the police raided
  his shotgun house. We relieved our knees

to lift our palms, surrender-style, fated.
  We could rub the cross-wire patterns off

but the smell of iron stuck to us
  and hasn't faded.

Silver City, New Mexico

Morning opens like a sore
                    in Silver City, where men
gut their own mother's
                    belly—not for precious metals

                    but truck loads of gravel
                                        for driveways, foundations,
            xeriscaped yards trying
                                so hard to look like they are

                                self-sufficient. The sun
            overtakes the sky, like pain
                                evaporates the mind and
            its little headlamp. A riddle:

what can be divided like a worm,
                    squirms, welcomes itself into one
body, is alive three times, you
                    would exchange a ton of gold

                                for any measure of it if you only knew
            it was leaving. I bet you got it
                                by now, I bet you guessed water.
            You'd be right. But I wasn't

thinking water. I thought God
                                or universe. Not that I'm wrong
or right to think this way,
                                because perception is on that list,

too. It fractures and isn't broken.

My neighbor in his 70's trailer

has about ten dogs, and those dogs

are believers, too, followers of the cult

of the Virgin of Pain. Their master

punishes them with a baseball bat for shitting

in the fenced-in yard. The bat is the metal kind

that rings across the exposed rock

as it strikes them across the back.
And the dogs don't break, neither

does the bat. They are the kindest dogs,

they fear their own bodies, bringers

of pain, because they know their bodies

are imperfect, defecate

when they meant to pray/fetch/

bone. It's hard to know what wise men

know. No, what wise men want

with such a limited brain. I wake to work

in the mines, well, to move

the gravel around, that's all I do all day.

It's what my father did, it's what my sons will do

unless they leave. We got rid of the old

trucks, the kind that dump by lifting back

in one huge pile. Now the truck bed

opens up in flaps like an autopsy,

disembowels itself. It's easy enough.

Still, I'll wake up grating

my teeth. There are more shards of meth

next door in Hurley than there are stars in the sky.

               But maybe we could all be good

if we could learn to be afraid

               of our own assholes. Sometimes

               when I wake, I could swear

                     someone was there. God, my mind

               leaps up—and I'm like a dog

                     jerked awake by its own fart.

Each morning, I wake up grateful.

               Each morning, I forget to remember

to call the dog pound. When I tell Marcelino,

               I swear to God, one of these days

                     I'm gunna do it, he only says: *sure you will.*

                     And day makes a fist, and parts

               of Silver City spill into the far away suburbs:

                     Santa Fe—Phoenix—Albuquerque—

Self-Portrait as a Man-Made Diamond

"Your very own LifeGem diamond can be created
from the carbon in cremation ashes, a lock of hair."
—WWW.LIFEGEM.COM

Clarity might be a virtue,
especially where diamonds

are concerned. But I am not
a diamond yet. I could be

burned in a pyre, release
periodic bonds, post bail.

Near nothing, I could be
pressured into permanence,

do the great "I do" dare, cannonball
into the infinity pool—

if I gave my warmth up,
if I agreed to live

in that permafrost
of forever, where nothing

is able to leave
a footprint or a scratch

because there is nothing for me
in immortality's tundra

to even chip my teeth on. I couldn't
live that way now, much less

after. Composure
and bling have never been

my thing. The only boots I've
ever owned were for work, not dance.

And I've always been of the mind
that if butter and bacon

make everything better, lard
makes everything best. Lard

that clarifies the pastry
bag, that clarifies the taste

of the pastry. That's my kind
of diamond, opaque but

dismisses opacity, can make
a damn good cake. Like fat,

I'm not pig-headed, though
I came from pigs. Solid

at room temp, keeps tempo
with the climate. Universal,

in other words, useful. Trust me,
if I were reduced to diamond

I'd be of such a quality
no one would want me—

but dentists would wield me
in their drill bits, their burrs.

Heart Conceit

As a boxer's punch begins in his feet,
my defeat begins when you unlace

my bootstraps, as if each foot were a gift
and you didn't want to rip the paper. As if

my mother made me this
body for you, not me. I slipped the knot

of my mother-tether more than twenty
rings ago, and I do feel duped, feel left

with that nameless zero since. I do
and I do and I do,

if you manage to toss a dime into my heart chalice—
if your dart can pin my center, if you can rope me

in the ring toss, or gun-stun my lucky duck. It's skill
that fillets the chicken into the chicken dinner

winner! Winner, maybe your practiced hands
could take my foot and find a rose

budding in the warped, white pucker of a plantar
wart. Celebrate each morning with our body-made

confetti   rustled up from dandruff, from agitated
dermatitis. Let's let fallout fall! Can't a calla lily be

the occasion for a calla lily? I want to be the opal
miner that mines your opal. Now, a ruby. Now,

harden your carbon to diamond. Facet your eyes
in bold-framed glasses, Urkel-like, my jeweler's loupe,

to magnify the magnificent otherwise missed.
The veining on the back of your hand is rising

beautifully, like the veins on a leaf. Own it.
Don't be ashamed to wear your gray hair

like tinsel or inlay. I will lick down
your cowlick and be your cow,

if you will be the milkweed
to my monarch—be the fig queen

who rips out her own wings
gnawing a path

to my chamber.

Gay Epithalamium

Girls, never ask your gay best friend when they're getting married. Never call your
gay best friend *your gay best friend*. Boys and girls, never ask your gay friends *who
is the woman and who is the man?* Because that's the whole point, we may act like a
lady but we don't care for the lady parts. Boys, if you mean to ask *who is the bottom
and who is the top?* I hope you know that asking this demonstrates interest in being
one of the two. One of the two. Boys and girls. Listen to me, still breaking up
with old black and white habits. When you mail your acceptance, please check if
you prefer the beef or fish. In English, beef can also mean to have a problem with.
In Spanish, a fish has been called *el que por la boca muere.* When I have a problem
I spit it out. Chicken isn't a menu option. My mouth has gotten my teeth knocked
out before—can you guess which? Don't assume I will get married. *But love is love.*
My tongue is in my cheek again, because where else would it be? Love is love, you
say, as if the heart were a palindrome. Friends, don't pretend orientation doesn't
matter. Or do these two sound the same to you: *This cake is to die for. // Is this the
cake I died for?* No, I don't care if a calla lily isn't a true lily. I would still include it
in my bouquet; I would stick it in your centerpiece anyway. You want to
know why I haven't gotten married? There aren't enough kinds of lilies: tiger, calla,
Easter, Asiatic, of the valley. Or maybe I don't think a Mary should get married,
anchored to the past. Or maybe because my partner can officiate a wedding for
his friends in 50 states, but a baker can still refuse to make our cake. It's an old
habit I still can't break. Thinking about getting gay married to my gay best friend,
praying to my gay God, having dinner with my gay family, using my gay hand
to spoon gay cake into my cake mouth. There aren't enough words for being gay:
fairy, pansy, sissy, and even cake. But also: confirmed bachelor, friend of Dorothy,
family. Why do you smash cake into your spouse's face on your wedding day? You
don't have to answer. Because my tongue is in my cheek again. Where else could it go?
I'm asking for a friend.

Huitlacoche

Go ahead and call me what I am,
                     call me: faggot, homo, joto, pinche puto.
Unhusk me if you must, call me
                     acquired, call me dirty, call me corn smut.

Though it looks like a prostate rolled in soot, huitlacoche
                     at the farmer's market sells as Mexican Truffle.
Yet farmers in your heartland treat it like a sickness.
                     And because disease can decimate a monoculture,

they are afraid. That's why they bundle and they burn it,
                     a literal faggot. I said it and I'll say it.
Call me what I am, and if you can't pronounce
                     my surname, I'm supposed to say don't sweat it.

Don't sweat it, because even huitlacoche is a corruption
                     of the Nahuatl cuitlacochin, which is a corruption
of cuitlacochi. Tongues make mistakes
                     and mistakes

make languages. Like I was saying, for a long time
                     I couldn't pronounce them either, the things I like.
As with any delicacy, it's best
                     to start slow. Sound it out. Huit—

la—co—che, an—u—lin—gus, mas—
                     tur—ba—tion. When you master
saying them out loud, it's time to rub any two
                     syllables together: cock, suck; pussy, fuck; ass, lick.

Relax. They are only words. They are the only words
        you need to insult someone
or to have sex with them
        no matter what country you find yourself in.

Words have their luggage like immigrants
        have their customs. Huitlacoche, mariposa, maricón.
Now that I have put it in my mouth,
        I am proud to be a faggot.

But it sounds so hateful when you say it.
        A coworker really said this to me. I said
because that's the way I always heard it.
        How do you speak such good English anyway?

Smile—say nothing—don't sweat it—he aimed it as a compliment.
        Faggot, wetback, huitlacoche, all my life I've heard it.
Learning English, *it hurted* is what I would say
        when I wanted to say *it hurt.* Not anymore. I know

all about tense agreement, just tell me where to conjugate
        and I will. Shut your mouth—when I'm talking
spores come out in droves like mosquitos
        birthed for blood—or I'll give you what I got.

Ode to the Touch-Me-Not

In the language of consent // I revoke // in the affirmative
but I'll tender for you an enthusiastic // get bent // my body

isn't up for debate // so you can go // shave your palms now
drop dead // bitch I might // take a page from female dragonflies

that fall on their backs // spread their legs // and wait for the man
to go the fuck away // but with my luck // he'd be a necrophiliac

creeps will touch you // and touch you // and touch you
and then // they'll claim that it's not true // movement

just your common // hydropump action // an easy trick
turgid and ready // and even came // loose with the swipe of a finger

they'll call you beautiful // they'll call you and call you // until
you relent or rebuff // their advances // claim they climbed into your pants

regardless // call you // coy cloister closet case cunt my mistake
if ever I made any // was not being carnivorous enough // nontoxic

or maybe not remaining my own // flowering clusterfuck // self-pollination
as a form of self-suck // this is a man's true fear // to be not needed

they'll swing your head // by your hair // and call it snakes
the blood that drops // a new genus // of undiscovered poppies

named for some cis het white // halfwit // who would and should have died
without help from the first people // who had their own name for this // rape

so they call me // a touch-me-not // dormilona when I'm wide awake
holgazana // can you believe it // when I'm paying his goddamn light bill

it was a man // of course it was a man // who named forget-me-nots
forget-me-nots // who can remember his pathetic name now // not me

The Language in Question

defying gravity after all // isn't the same as flying

after all // are you thinking of hurting yourself

isn't the same as are you thinking // you might kill

yourself // we must be confident being more

direct // an X drawn in orange on a tree trunk

one morning it was there // 30 feet of maple

gone by the time I came back home // the city

gave me no choice // sometimes we have no choice

and warning signs can go unnoticed // until I didn't

think they were serious // they wanted attention

didn't mean it sometimes it doesn't hurt // death

feels like a solution // sometimes it hurts so much

after all // you are thinking of hurting yourself no

you are thinking of hurting // other people not us

walking a gorge late at night // leaves rustle their

should I live and should I live // no one wants to die

are you nobody too // good then we're not alone

please don't die // it's good advice I don't want

my kind of sadness // is like my favorite tree

planted long before me // shadow punctured now

and then with light // when gusts ghost through

and that's enough for me // the garden thrived

except the lilies planted in full sun // didn't make it

I planted a new tree // in the hollow of what I had lost

one day I'll rest in its shade // should I live that long

Keeping Home

Together, we almost compete with the chores
of keeping home. But this isn't what we intended
years ago when we said to each other "you complete me."
We got monkey's pawed in love, you see.
Well, mostly you. You have a large
heart. It sounds sweet unless it's
a doctor who says it. Your cardiologist said, "at least
we can rule out pregnancy," you said, "unless
we count the agita, ulcer, kidney stone, take
your pick. This sucks. We're falling apart
growing old together." Somewhere between
the aisle with orthopedic inserts and the one with
hemorrhoid cream, fine, my love, I see what you mean.
But we are growing old, *and* we are growing
together, like the wild vine along our fence
that, nameless, appeared to have been planted
overnight, when in truth it fed on our neglect,
crept, link by link, until it was the only thing,
link by link, holding the fence together. And, petty,
when the neighbors called it a nuisance, we
watered it—in spite of inedible berries, despite it
choking out the lilacs. We called it "kind of pretty."
In this hotter than normal June, on this hotter than
normal planet, I'll pull the weeds like electrical plugs,
and if I croak from heat stroke, say I was your one and only
monkey's paw. You mow the lawn and gut the gutters and
maybe at your eulogy I'll say he had the largest heart.

Ode to Adam Rippon's Butt

In the language of the body // merci for this grand bounty // I have to say olé
to that Olympic butt in a way that isn't crass // so here's your VIP full access // pass

to that show stopper // champagne top popper // better wear your best seersucker
because sure Adam's feet flow like cursive // but let's be honest // what freak

nun is looking at your feet // with a booty that says goddamn // I believe in God
I'm a follower // a convert to your corvette vroom // zooming in suit that says

eat me // the way you scarf down a double-decker burger // dripping with juices
in full carnal knowledge // it's no good for you // but you stuff your face anyway

without reservation // and even Five Guys // isn't out of the question
did I mention // the special is a buy-one-get-one // free to hair-flip online haters

spin in high heels // strike a pose or gag on Gaga // in a sequin laser light show
with disco washboard stomach // or red carpet ready // dashing in your leather harness

answering what's it like to be a gay // athlete in a sport so vehemently // straight-
up homophobic are you still surprised // I'm not // it's the same as anywhere

and always // but with better eyebrows // it's like you're Madonna classic telling
reporters you're a basic // Catholic schoolgurl bia-tch // sassy & saucy & cheeky

to the chin // if the Pope wants to see me let him // buy a ticket like anyone else
does anyone else think about hell // missing an angel // because a butt like that

was made for falling // what cushion to soften the blow // I know I'm hard
crushing ice chips with my teeth // I don't care // just look at that derriere

is it really so terrible // to just this one time let us have this // yes homo yes
me why should I care // what one more glittering fairy has to add // it's sad

that's the discourse of some guys // think it doesn't matter // that he's gay
it matters out in public // at the doctor's office // it matters it matters

to the men who would beat him // and he might get beaten // in technique
Adam said as much but no one turns a cheek // like me // smeared in Vice

President Pence's rhetorical smatter // don't tell me // it doesn't matter
so this is an ode // to Adam Rippon's butt // go ahead and call it shallow

the rink is so // because it needs to be // hell hath frozen over and I'm here
making angels out of snow with a fury // to jump high // first crouch low

ACKNOWLEDGEMENTS

Grateful acknowledgements to the editors of the journals where these poems first appeared:

85 South Journal // "Mourning Dove"

AGNI // "Ode to Adam Rippon's Butt"

American Poetry Review // "Ode to the Pitcher Plant," "This Way to the Egress" (as "The Egress"), "The Language in Question" [He has a mouth on him.], "The Language in Question" [When I called you a beluga whale,] and "The Language in Question" [Defying gravity after all]

Boston Review // "Ode to the Corpse Flower"

Crazyhorse // "Self-Portrait as a Man-Made Diamond"

Foglifter // "Mutual Monogamy"

Four Way Review // "A Toast to the Destruction of Sodom and Gomorra"

Four Way Review // "Reasons for Abolishing Ice" (as "Reasons for Distrusting Ice")

Gulf Coast // "A Father's Portrait in Styrofoam"

Ithaca Lit // "Queso de patas" (as "La Güera")

Kenyon Review // "The Great Glass Closet," "Warrior Song," and "Le daría mis pulmones"

Lambda Literary // "Conversations with My Father"

The Missouri Review // "Anti-Ode to the Man-O-War" and "Keeping Home"

New England Review // "Ode to the Peacock"

Newfound // "To the Unborn Sibling"

Nimrod International // "Gay Epithalamium"

Palette Poetry // "Huitlacoche"

[PANK] // "On the Slight Cruelty of Mothers"

Plume // "Nonmonogamy"

Poet Lore // "The Memory Jar"

Poets.org (Poem a Day) // "Bliss Point or What Can Best Be Achieved by Cheese"

Prairie Schooner // "Heroin with an E"

Puerto del Sol // "The Language in Question" [The language in question is criminal]

RHINO // "The Darkest Lashes"
Tinderbox Poetry Journal // "Eye of the Hurricane" and "Silver City, New Mexico"
West Branch Wired // "Heart Conceit"

Thank you to the editors of the following venues that gave these poems another home:
200 New Mexico Poems // "The Memory Jar"
BreakBeat Poets Vol. 4: LatiNEXT // "The Language in Question" [The language in question is criminal] and "Ode to the Peacock"
Best New Poets 2016 // "Le daría mis pulmones"
Best New Poets 2018 // "Ode to the Corpse Flower"
Foglifter (blog) // "Huitlacoche"
Los hijos de Whitman // "A Father's Portrait in Styrofoam" (as "Retrato de padre en poliestireno")
The Slowdown // "Bliss Point of What Can Best Be Achieved by Cheese"
Verse Daily // "Heroin with an E"

Thank you: Kazim Ali, for your faith, courage, and generosity.

Thank you: to the remarkable folks at Milkweed Editions (with special thanks to Lee Oglesby and Daniel Slager).

Thank you: all of the folks involved in the National Poetry Series, for this opportunity.

Thank you: Sally Wen Mao, Eduardo C. Corral, and Danez Smith, for lending me your kind words.

Thank you: Benjamín García (not me, the artist featured on the cover), for gracing my book with your work, and Mary Austin Speaker, for bringing it all together.

Thank you: all of the hardworking folks at the following institutions that provided me space, guidance, funding, community, and other forms of support I hope to one day pay forward:

CantoMundo, The Frost Place, Lambda Literary, The Palm Beach Poetry Festival, Bread Loaf Writer's Conference, Taos Sumer Writer's Conference, The National Latino Writer's Conference, the National Hispanic Cultural Center, the University of New Mexico, and Cornell University.

Thank you: Trillium Health for allowing me to learn so much about myself by teaching others. Without these experiences, this book would not be possible. Thank you especially: Dr. Valenti, Michael Lecker, Kristen MacKay, Julie Ritzler, and Emily Smith.

Thank you to all of my MFA instructors: Alice Fulton, for your keen eyes. Lyrae Van Clief-Stefanon, for showing me how to "eat the fish and spit out the bones." Kenneth McLane, for your unwavering encouragement. Stephanie Vaughn and Helena María Viramontes, thank you for being such strong advocates for your students.

Thank you for your support: Maudelle Driskell, Patrick Donnelly, Gabrielle Calvocoressi, Joy Harjo, Amy Beeder, Valerie Martínez, Jack Trujillo, Ross Gay, Yona Harvey, Martha Collins, Martín Espada, Diane Thiel, Martha Rhodes, Edward Hirsch, Rigoberto González, Javier Zamora, and Natalie Scenters-Zapico.

Thank you: Dana Levin, for being a force of good. For believing in me when I couldn't.

Thank you: Mrs. Price, Stephanie Hobbs, Yvette Hines, Michael Pérez, and James Raines for fanning a small fire. And to you, Brenda Huerta, Lynda Le, Lisa Marie Ramírez, for standing with me.

Thank you to my community of writers: Tacey Atsitty, Elizabeth Lindsey Rogers, Tanaya Winder, Joy Priest, Justin Jannise, and _____ (for the name I have surely forgotten). All my love to the Ironclad Medusa Collective: Mandy Gutmann-Gonzalez, Liza Flum, and Emily Oliver. A special thank you to the folks who put up with my annoying excitement at a new draft, often my first readers: Alex Chertok, Christopher Phelps, Suzanne Richardson, and Casandra Lopez.

Thank you: to all the women, queer, Latinx, trans, black, marginalized writers whose voices have guided me to mine, and whose work has made mine possible.

Thank you: to all of my family, chosen and not. Thank you especially to Mario, for always watching out for me. Thank you Miguel, for surviving with me. Thank you to my dad, for trying. Thank you to Jorge, Ernesto, Chantel, Marlene, Darlene, Perfecto. Thank you, Uncle Andy, for always encouraging us to create. Thank you, Bessettes, for being so welcoming.

Thank you: Nana, for your strength/wisdom/love. For randomly saying to an eleven-year-old boy, "Ricky Martin is gay and that's okay."

Thank you: Nick, for adding music to my life.

Amá: gracias por todo, qué suerte la mía.

Thrown in the Throat is dedicated to anyone who has lived in a closet. It sucks. I'm sorry. I'm here, in this book, with you.

And you, reader, thank you for opening this book.

Lynda Le *photography*

BENJAMIN GARCIA was a 2019 Lambda Literary Fellow, the 2017 Latinx Scholar at the Frost Place, and a 2018 CantoMundo Fellow at the Palm Beach Poetry Festival. His work has appeared in *American Poetry Review*, *Best New Poets 2018*, *Crazyhorse*, *Kenyon Review*, *the Missouri Review*, and *New England Review*. Garcia received his MFA from Cornell University and currently works as a sexual health and harm reduction educator in the Finger Lakes region of New York.

milkweed
editions

Founded as a nonprofit organization in 1980,
Milkweed Editions is an independent publisher. Our mission
is to identify, nurture and publish transformative literature,
and build an engaged community around it.

milkweed.org

Interior design by Mary Austin Speaker
Typeset in Adobe Caslon
by Mary Austin Speaker

Adobe Caslon Pro was created by Carol Twombly
for Adobe Systems in 1990. Her design was inspired by
the family of typefaces cut by the celebrated engraver
William Caslon I, whose family foundry served
England with clean, elegant type from the early
Enlightenment through the turn of the
twentieth century.